Done With Dieting!

An Inspirational Journal Exploring Emotional Eating

BETSY LOU ZIPKIN

BALBOA.PRESS

A DIVISION OF HAY HOUSE

Balboa Press books may be ordered through booksellers or by contacting:

Balboa Press
A Division of Hay House
1663 Liberty Drive
Bloomington, IN 47403
www.balboapress.com
1 (877) 407-4847

Because of the dynamic nature of the Internet, any web addresses or
links contained in this book may have changed since publication and
may no longer be valid. The views expressed in this work are solely those
of the author and do not necessarily reflect the views of the publisher,
and the publisher hereby disclaims any responsibility for them.

The author of this book does not dispense medical advice or prescribe the use
of any technique as a form of treatment for physical, emotional, or medical
problems without the advice of a physician, either directly or indirectly. The
intent of the author is only to offer information of a general nature to help
you in your quest for emotional and spiritual well-being. In the event you use
any of the information in this book for yourself, which is your constitutional
right, the author and the publisher assume no responsibility for your actions.

Any people depicted in stock imagery provided by Getty Images are
models, and such images are being used for illustrative purposes only.
Certain stock imagery © Getty Images.

Print information available on the last page.

ISBN: 978-1-9822-3827-8 (sc)
ISBN: 978-1-9822-3828-5 (e)

Balboa Press rev. date: 11/12/2019

1

I am not a number on a scale,
Or how I may appear to others,
I am always uniquely me,
Looking to give and to receive Divine Love.

2

"My relationship with food
Is my relationship with myself." *(author unknown)*

3

My relationship with food does reflect
My relationship with myself,
And also my relationship with Source.

4

*I want my relationship with myself to be
Kind instead of critical.
Supportive rather than dismissive.*

5

"All bodily appetites are really a yearning for God."
(A Course In Miracles) ©
We are always reaching out to feel Divine Love.

6

Will I be guided by Love or fear today
As I make my food choices?
Love's choices are much more satisfying.

§

7

My struggles with food
Are really about facing all my feelings,
Even uncomfortable ones.

8

When I overeat, it's just an attempt
To avoid unpleasant feelings.
That can be a big realization.

9

If I have a hunger in my heart that needs to be satisfied,
The real nourishment I need is from my own self-love.

10

It is possible to see food as an ally, rather than an adversary.

When I do, I will be able to savor and enjoy each meal and snack.

Regret and guilt will be set aside and put on the back burner.

11

If I do give in to some food temptation today,
How will I treat myself later?
When food becomes an ally rather than adversary,
Forgiveness becomes an option to be chosen.

12

I tell myself today:
"Everything I eat and drink,
Contributes to my good health, well-being, and my
perfect weight of_____."
(Sondra Ray, (The Forgiveness Diet-The Only Diet
There Is.)

13

Instead of immediately eating, if I feel bored today,
I stop and take a few gentle, deep breaths,
And then decide-what and how much I will eat.

14

What is the difference between emotional and physical hunger?

One is fueled by an emptiness of the heart.

And perhaps, a need for instant gratification.

The other can be more easily satisfied.

And even reasonable about when to have the next snack or meal.

15

When I feel filled with peace and well-being,
My physical hunger is more easily satisfied.
And I gravitate towards healthier food choices.

16

*Is there one thing I do like about my appearance?
If not, is there one quality about the 'inner me'
I do feel pleased about?*

17

If I want a new relationship with food,
I need to talk to myself in a soothing way.
For example: "It really is ok to like myself,
No matter what anyone else may think, feel,
or say about my weight or appearance."

18

I can also admit I don't like myself,
If others are not approving of me in some way.
Honesty matters.

19

I need to remember today that emotional hunger is
Yearning for a satisfaction, that goes beyond
The temporary comfort of food.

20

There is nothing wrong with using food as a temporary comfort ;
What is really helpful is to allow and embrace my feelings more,
And turn less often to food for relief.

21

How do I go about allowing and embracing my feelings?
The first step is just deciding to do so.
And sincerely making that commitment.

22

Giving myself permission to feel-
Without censoring myself- can ease
a lot of hunger pains!

23

I can love and accept myself,
No matter what my emotional state may be.
Running away from feelings, keeps me stuck.

24

As I allow and embrace my feelings
More and more,
I will start to turn
Less and less,
To food for comfort.

25

*I invite Source to guide
And take care of
All food issues today.*

26

When I feel alone
Or lonely in the world,
I can allow Source to direct me,
To the non-food alternative
I am really looking for.

27

*Today, I begin to explore the
Connection between overeating,
Holding grievances, and a need to forgive.*

28

When I judge anyone, including myself-
My heart seems to shut down.
And turning to food feels like a comfort.
Instead, I could decide to open my heart.

29

Learning to be forgiving with myself,
When I do overeat, or not eat enough,
Will replace any judgmental or critical feeling.

30

When I truly acknowledge all my emotions,
There will be no need to binge and try to
Devour my feelings.

31

Liking myself, no matter
what food choices I may make,
Is a giant step forward
in feeling the worthiness within..

32

Forgiveness is a Divine Solution,
Because it changes my relationship
With food from negative and distressing,
To positive and Faith filled.

33

Giving up grievances affects all areas of my life.
It makes room for the realizations;
"people are either acting loving or
reaching out for love." (A Course In Miracles) ©

34

When I exercise, instead of eat,
I allow more time to get in touch with-
The uncomfortable feelings-
I may be trying to avoid.

35

Avoiding or invalidating feelings
Never really works.
Being authentic with myself always does.

36

My relationship with food,
Always does reflect
My relationship with myself.
How would I describe that relationship today?

37

Eating without guilt, shame, or worry,
Is the way I want my life to be.
And I deserve it.

38

I want to breathe slowly and with awareness,
During each meal today and genuinely appreciate,
Whatever I may choose to eat.

39

Today I want to relax, take time to
Consciously breathe, and nourish
Myself in ways unrelated to food.

40

Nourishing myself can take many forms.
Journaling is one way that also can connect me
To what is happening in my head and heart.
I am thankful for the Peace it can bring.

41

Communicating and connecting
More deeply with others
Provides another opportunity for
Nurturing myself without food.

42

Its really not so much about
The quantity of food I consume,
As it is about treating my body
And myself with respect..

43

Can I be satisfied with less,
Rather than more around food?
Try this mindfulness exercise: Take one raisin, see how long
You can chew and enjoy the taste. (John Cabot Zinn)

44

Love is the inner food
I am searching for.
And it is always available to me,
Because it comes from My Source.

45

What are three things I appreciate around food ?
I decide to have an attitude of savoring,
Rather than worry, around all my food choices today,

46

Obsessing about my
Weight or appearance,
Serves no useful purpose.
Being kind to myself will.

47

Which do I value more?
How I look on the outside,
Or feel on the inside?

48

If I feel disappointed in myself,
I take a minute, breathe slowly,
And acknowledge that feeling as ok.
Now I can decide if and what I will eat.

49

I decide what and how much
To eat-every day.
Whether to diet is always my choice.
Divine Counsel is always available.
To guide me to my best self-care.

50

There are no formulas or rules around food.
Other than the ones I choose.
Everything comes down to someone's opinion.
I will let my heart lead me.

51

Taking time to be in touch
With my feelings each day,
Is a very nourishing thing to do.

52

How do I feel about the kind of
Nutrition I receive each day?
Spiritual, emotional, and physical care matter.
Trusting myself around food
Is always possible. Because of
The Divine Food Counselor that
Always walks beside me.

53

It is a a lack of forgiveness
I have towards myself,
That needs to be revealed.
So I may be healed of an
Inner starvation.

54

If I feel concerned about others
Judging my appearance, it really is
M own self wrath, I am trying to escape.

55

When I blame others or myself
For what seems lacking in my life,
I am choosing a path of
Bitterness and resentment.

56

*The antidote to bitterness and resentment
Is forgiveness, in large quantities.
And that will taste very good.*

57

When I taste harmony more fully in my life,
I will be fulfilled on a level that food
Cannot cater to.

58

I do want to be satisfied by food, without overeating.
More food does not mean more fulfillment in my life.
Neither does eating too little.

59

What role does conflict play in
When and how much I eat?
I notice today the times I turn to
Food for comfort or escape.

60

Noticing how often I turn
To resolve conflict with food,
Is a first step towards more harmony.

61

I decide today to spend more
Time resolving upset in ways
Other than eating.

62

There is no need to judge myself
For avoiding upsets or resentments
By over-eating or undereating.

63

Today I allow myself to feel any upsets,
And stop before reacting,
With some gentle, deep breaths.

64

Breathing into any negative feeling,
and sitting quietly as soon as possible.
Allows the feeling to pretty quickly dissipate.

65

It feels safe to turn to food often,
Because it is so familiar.
New patterns of eating
Can become second nature as well.

66

It may seem too simplistic,
But loving myself
And whatever food I may eat,
Can only contribute to my well-being!

67

When I genuinely value myself,
I just naturally gravitate,
Towards more loving eating.

68

What does it mean to eat more lovingly?
To genuinely appreciate and savor
All meals and snacks, and make
Delicious and nutritious food choices.

69

*Respecting myself plays
An important role
In all my choices
Food and otherwise.*

70

I want to cultivate a sense of ease
And peace in my life.
And stop worrying about how
I may look to others!

71

When I feel happy with myself,
I could crave less sugar.
I am ready to put my own sweetness into my life.

72

Being kinder to myself reduces stress.
Less stress equals less focus on food
As a problem solver.

73

Letting myself be more authentically me,
Is a big help in turning within,
Rather than without for comfort.

74

All external searching for comfort is not bad,
It's just not particularly helpful
In dealing with food issues.

75

If not eating enough or
Taking time to eat, when
Feeling upset is an issue,
I remember food is here
To help, not harm me.

76

Here's a good food tip:
Drink one full glass of water
Before eating dinner,
And it will be easy to consume less food.

77

Its not so much about overeating,
As it is about how I feel about myself,
If I overeat.

78

Its also not so much about what I eat,
As it is about feeling guilty if I'm not
Meeting self-expectations.

79

"*Beware of the temptation to perceive yourself unfairly treated*"
(*A Course In Miracles*) ©
This can be a big justification for soothing myself
With a food reward.

80

Instead of blaming another, when things
Are not working out according to my plan-
I want to open myself to see new
Loving perspectives.

81

There are so many ways to see or interpret
What is happening in my life.
I notice how letting go of blame
Affects my eating patterns today.

82

When I am more responsive and
Less reactive to others, I feel better.
And when I feel better, I can make
More Loving food choices.

83

Making loving food choices is taking
Good care of myself. It is a loving choice
To decide not to overeat.

§

84

I want to like myself
Whether I do or do not
Overeat or undereat.

85

Do I treat myself the same around food
Whether at home or out socializing?
Which could be more of a challenge for me?
Why?

86

When I can really be ok with any feeling,
I will also be ok with food and myself,
Whether at home or out socially.

87

Soothing myself with food is
Temporary pleasure for what
Can feel like ongoing emotional pain.

88

I can look forward to a present,
That is happier and more peaceful
Than anything I have ever experienced.

89

What is a no-nonsense attitude
Towards weight-control? It is
A permissive attitude to be
Who I really am!

90

Is there a connection
Between waiting-on
People with resentment,
And putting on weight?
Yes, there is!

91

I just notice today
How often I turn towards food,
When I feel insecure
About pleasing another.

92

When I reduce the amount of anger,
Towards others or myself,
I will also lower the number of
Pounds in my belly.

93

Avoiding upset or angry feelings
Can affect my desire to eat in general.
Or to get rid of the food I do.

94

Its really important when I'm feeling 'fed up'
With a person or situation,
Not to start feeding myself.
I need to just be with the anger
And My Higher Power.

95

When I censor my feelings,
I censor myself,
And then I will probably
Turn to food for relief.

96

I ask myself today:
What is one thing I am proud of
Around food? What is one thing I could
Compliment myself about in general?

97

If I only like myself based on
How I look, or what I am eating-
I'm being unkind to me.

98

When I feel pleased about doing
Something well, do I give myself
A food treat as a reward?

99

When I shut down inside,
It puts my feelings in the freezer.
When will I let myself "Thaw out"?

100

Appearances may change,
Numbers on a scale go up and down.
Divine Love is always a constant.

101

No amount of calorie counting
Or food watching, will replace
The satisfaction of living each day
With a passionate purpose.

102

When I allow myself to feel
all my emotions, I am healing
My relationship with food.